D1408410

SPOTLIGHT ON SOCIAL AND EMOTIONAL LEARNING

THOUGHTS AND FEELINGS

IDENTIFYING EMOTIONS

RACHAEL MORLOCK

PowerKiDS press.

NEW YORK

Published in 2020 by The Rosen Publishing Group, Inc.
29 East 21st Street, New York, NY 10010

Copyright © 2020 by The Rosen Publishing Group, Inc.

All rights reserved. No part of this book may be reproduced in any form without permission in writing from the publisher, except by a reviewer.

Editor: Elizabeth Krajnik
Designer: Michael Flynn

Photo Credits: Cover JGI/Jamie Grill/Blend Images/Getty Images; cover, pp. 1, 3, 4, 6, 8, 10, 12, 14, 16, 18, 20, 22–24 (background) TairA/Shutterstock.com; p. 5 ZoneCreative/Shutterstock.com; p. 7 (Dalai Lama) Nadezda Murmakova/Shutterstock.com; p. 7 (Paul Ekman) Steven Dewall/Redferns/Getty Images; p. 9 (background) Konstantin Zubarev/Shutterstock.com; p. 9 (tree) mirrelley/Shutterstock.com; p. 11 Thiago Bernardes/LightRocket/Getty Images; p. 12 ESB Professional/Shutterstock.com; p. 13 Lapina/Shutterstock.com; p. 15 Kevin Mazur/Getty Images Entertainment/Getty Images; p. 17 Nick Dolding/Cultura/Getty Images; p. 18 wavebreakmedia/Shutterstock.com; p. 19 Artbox/Shutterstock.com; pp. 20–21 Jabin Botsford/The Washington Post/Getty Images; p. 22 LightField Studios/Shutterstock.com.

Cataloging-in-Publication Data

Names: Morlock, Rachael.
Title: Thoughts and feelings: identifying emotions / Rachael Morlock.
Description: New York : PowerKids Press, 2020. | Series: Spotlight on social and emotional learning | Includes glossary and index.
Identifiers: ISBN 9781725302112 (pbk.) | ISBN 9781725302303 (library bound) | ISBN 9781725302211 (6pack)
Subjects: LCSH: Emotions--Juvenile literature. | Emotions in children--Juvenile literature.
Classification: LCC BF723.E6 M67 2020 | DDC 152.4--dc23

Manufactured in the United States of America

CPSIA Compliance Information: Batch #CSPK19. For further information contact Rosen Publishing, New York, New York at 1-800-237-9932.

CONTENTS

CHAPTER ONE

WHAT ARE EMOTIONS?

Think about your first day of school. Can you remember how you felt? You might have been excited to see your friends, nervous to meet your teacher, or sad to be away from your parents. Maybe you had all those feelings at once!

Feelings are very personal reactions to an emotion. Everyone has emotions, no matter how old they are or where they live. Emotions can be signals with **information** about the world around us. They may give us an idea about whether something will be good or bad for us.

Emotions sometimes come quickly and unexpectedly. You might experience a jumble of emotions that change the way you think, the way your body feels, the way you look, and the way you act. With practice, you can learn to slow down, think about and name your emotions, and decide what to do next.

We can recognize emotions by the way they make us look and feel. This boy's **expressions** show different emotions. Can you guess what they are?

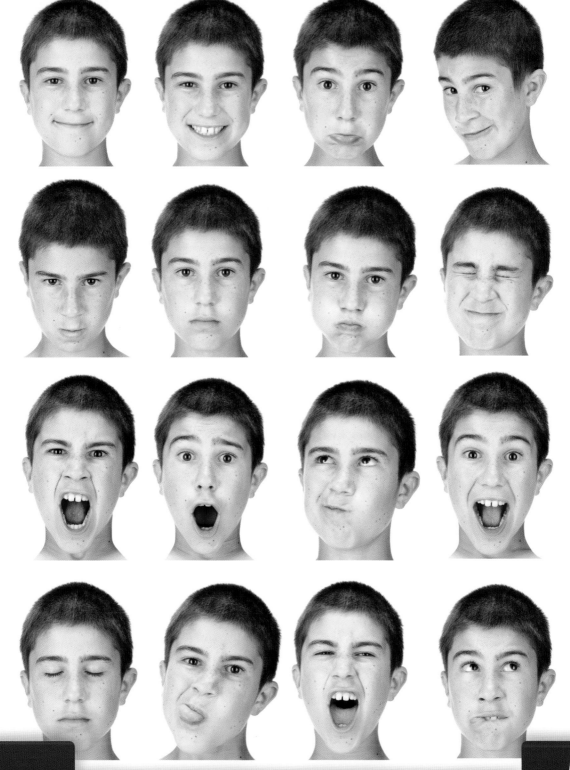

CHAPTER TWO

EMOTIONS MATTER

Even though some emotions are more enjoyable than others, emotions themselves are neither good nor bad. Emotions can tell us where we are in relation to our goals. Some emotions, such as anxiety, feel **negative**. They signal that we are blocked or moving away from our goals. Other emotions, like joy or peace, feel positive. They tell us that we are moving closer to our goals.

Both positive and negative emotions can give us helpful information. An emotion tells you that there's something important to pay attention to—something in your situation is causing your body and mind to react. Understanding why you feel different emotions can help you look more clearly for the source of the emotion. Then, you can choose how to **respond** to that information. Emotions provide clues about how to act so that we can move forward and make things better.

The Dalai Lama, a **Buddhist** leader, and **psychologist** Paul Ekman work together to teach people about emotions. They believe that understanding your emotions can make you more calm and healthy.

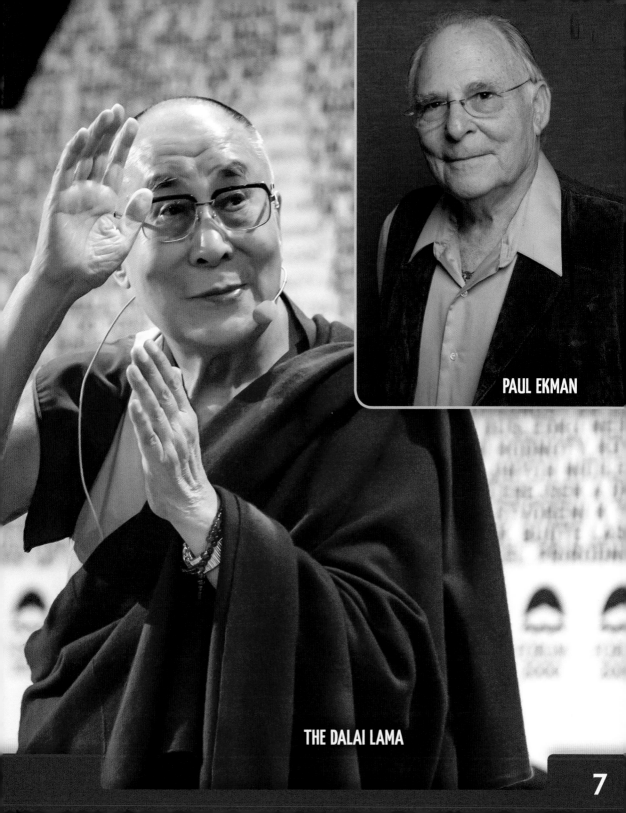

PAUL EKMAN

THE DALAI LAMA

CHAPTER THREE

SORTING EMOTIONS

An important step in understanding emotions is identifying them. There are hundreds of words to describe our feelings. Luckily, most emotions are related to each other. They can be put into a few simple groups.

Scientists and psychologists have discovered that at least four emotions are often recognized in similar ways around the world. Happiness, anger, fear, and sadness are considered **universal** emotions. Smiles often show happiness and frowns suggest anger. Other expressions show fear or sadness. These four emotions are a good place to begin when identifying your feelings.

You can think of happiness, anger, sadness, and fear as tree trunks with a number of similar emotions as branches. Usually, the emotions in each "tree" make you feel and act in similar ways. Some branches are large and strong while others are small and weaker.

Not all your emotions will fit into these four groups. Some are a mixture of more than one group. Others, like surprise, may form their own smaller group.

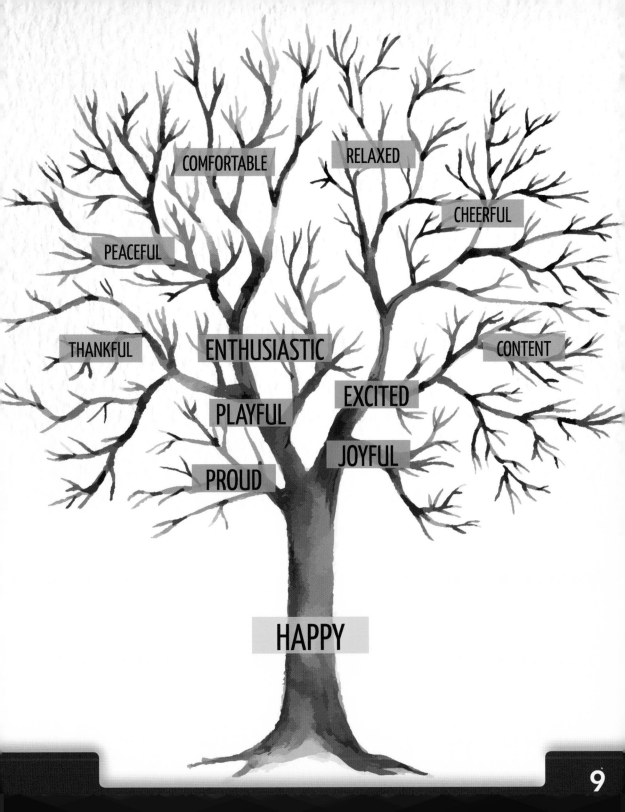

CHAPTER FOUR

HAPPINESS

Your favorite emotions probably fall into the happiness group. You can be content, relaxed, comfortable, thankful, cheerful, peaceful, joyful, or delighted. Happy emotions signal that things are going well as you move toward your goals.

How does happiness feel? You might have a feeling of warmth or a burst of energy. The way your voice sounds and the movements you make with your face and body provide clues about how you feel, too. Smiling and laughing are common signs of happiness.

What makes you happy? A positive experience with one of your five senses, like eating something delicious or taking a refreshing swim, can inspire happy emotions. You may also feel happy after an accomplishment or a connection with another person. To explore your happiness, ask yourself, "What goal am I moving toward? What is helping me get there?"

After defeating Croatia in the 2018 World Cup, the French team looked very happy! They might have also felt proud, energized, or relieved. What other emotions do you think they experienced?

CHAPTER FIVE

ANGER

Unlike happiness, anger is usually unpleasant. Rage and fury are more powerful than **irritation** and **annoyance**, but they are all related to anger. Other forms include grumpiness and **impatience**.

How does your body feel when you're angry? Anger can make you hot and uncomfortable. You might feel energy building up suddenly inside you as you get ready to act. Angry people often frown, turn red or pale, curl their hands into fists, cross their arms, or shout.

What clues tell you that these children are angry with each other? Pay attention to the positions of their bodies and the expressions on their faces.

Angry emotions come when you feel unfairly blocked on the path to your goals. You might be grumpy when a storm keeps you inside, annoyed when someone cuts ahead of you in line, or furious when a family member doesn't respect your privacy. When you feel angry, ask yourself, "What goal do I want to reach? What is blocking me?"

CHAPTER SIX

SADNESS

Sadness is another difficult, or hard to deal with, emotion to experience. **Disappointment**, **discouragement**, loneliness, hopelessness, sorrow, helplessness, and misery are all forms of sadness. Feelings of sadness are related to a sense of loss.

How can you tell when you're sad? Some people experience a heavy or tired feeling with sad emotions. Their bodies seem to droop. They might become quiet or turn away from people they love or things they usually enjoy. Tears are a common sign that someone is sad.

You have sad emotions when you have lost or will lose something or someone important to you. You may feel disappointment after losing a game, sorrow when a pet dies, or loneliness when a friend moves away. When you feel sad, ask yourself, "What have I lost? Why is it valuable to me?" These questions can help you deal with your sadness.

Emma González spoke at the March for Our Lives event on March 24, 2018. González shared her **grief** after losing friends in the Marjory Stoneman Douglas High School shooting in Parkland, Florida.

15

CHAPTER SEVEN

FEAR

Anxiety, nervousness, alarm, worry, **dread**, panic, and terror are emotions connected with fear. Fear comes from a sense that you are in danger. Fear can be very useful in keeping you safe. However, it can also stop people from trying new things.

What does fear feel like? Your body can respond very strongly to fear. Sometimes your heart races, you breathe quickly, your limbs and voice shake, your eyes open wide, and your muscles feel tight. Your body is creating a lot of energy in case you need to fight or run away to protect yourself.

We experience fear when it seems like a situation is risky for us. You might feel nervous about doing a class presentation, worried about your parents' relationship, or terrified of heights. If you're feeling fear, ask yourself, "What seems dangerous to me? Why?"

Getting to the bottom of your emotions is hard work! You might need to pay close attention what's happened to you in the past in order to understand your fear.

CHAPTER EIGHT

NAMING EMOTIONS

A good way to untangle your emotions is to find the right words to describe them. Start by telling the story of your emotions to a friend, a parent, or even yourself. If you're feeling upset, when did that feeling start? Where were you and what were you doing? What happened next? Ask yourself how you felt at the beginning, middle, and end of your story.

Not everyone experiences emotions the same way. Try keeping an emotion journal to help you track and recognize your emotions. Draw or write about the way your emotions look, feel, and sound.

If you're feeling stuck, you can use the four basic emotions to start describing your feelings. Think about how your body felt, the faces you were making, and the thoughts you had. Then, look for words that describe your emotions more exactly. Naming your emotions can help you tell others how you're feeling. The more you know about your emotions, the easier it will be to respond to them in healthy ways.

CHAPTER NINE

TAKING CHARGE

Emotions can be difficult guests in our minds and bodies. They often come uninvited and stay longer than we want. You can't choose which emotions you feel, but you can decide what to do with them. Although emotions aren't good or bad, our actions can be. Actions can hurt or help us and others.

One key to managing your emotions is practice. These fourth graders at Lafayette Elementary School in Washington, D.C., are practicing mindfulness in a special class.

    One way to slow down our emotions is to practice mindfulness. Mindfulness is paying attention to your thoughts and feelings in the present moment without judging them. It can give you time to name and understand your emotions before you act.

    As you learn more about your emotions, you can come up with positive ways to react to them. Try thinking of healthy responses to anger, sadness, happiness, or fear in your emotion journal. The next time you feel those emotions, choose one of the responses you came up with.

CHAPTER TEN

SHARING EMOTIONS

Knowing how to identify your emotions is an important ability. It gives you the tools to understand how you're feeling and why. These tools help you build your self-awareness—a true sense of who you are.

Identifying emotions also helps you to communicate and explain your feelings. When you talk with others about how you feel, you create new opportunities for solving problems. Sharing your emotions is a healthy and helpful way to deal with them.

Being able to identify your emotions also makes you better at identifying other people's emotions. Empathy is the ability to understand or imagine other people's experiences. An important part of empathy is noticing how people feel. Practicing empathy and learning to recognize and share your emotions can help you become a healthier person, a stronger member of your family and community, and even a better friend.

GLOSSARY

annoyance (uh-NOY-uhnts) A feeling of being bothered.

Buddhist (BOO-dist) A person who follows Buddhism, or a religion of eastern and central Asia that is based on the teachings of Guatama Buddha.

disappointment (dis-uh-POYNT-muhnt) A feeling of unhappiness because something hoped for or expected to happen failed to happen.

discouragement (dis-KUHR-ihj-muhnt) A feeling of being without courage or confidence.

dread (DREHD) A feeling of great fear, especially of something that will or might happen.

expression (ihk-SPREH-shuhn) The look on someone's face.

grief (GREEF) A feeling of very deep sorrow.

impatience (ihm-PAY-shuhnts) A feeling of restlessness or lack of patience.

information (ihn-fuhr-MAY-shuhn) Knowledge or facts about something.

irritation (ir-uh-TAY-shuhn) A feeling of displeasure, anger, or annoyance.

negative (NEH-guh-tiv) Harmful or bad, also unwanted.

psychologist (sy-KAH-luh-jist) A person who studies psychology, or the science or study of the mind and behavior.

respond (rih-SPAHND) To do something as a reaction to something that has happened or been done.

universal (yoo-nuh-VUHR-suhl) Done or experienced by everyone.

INDEX

PRIMARY SOURCE LIST

Page 7
Dalai Lama waving. Photograph. Nadezda Murmakova. October 19, 2016. Shutterstock.

Page 11
Players from France celebrate the 2018 World Cup title. Photograph. Thiago Bernardes. July 15, 2018. LightRocket, Pacific Press.

Page 15
Emma González speaks at March For Our Lives in Washington, D.C. Photograph. Kevin Mazur. March 24, 2018. Getty Images Entertainment, Getty Images North America.

WEBSITES

Due to the changing nature of Internet links, PowerKids Press has developed an online list of websites related to the subject of this book. This site is updated regularly. Please use this link to access the list: www.powerkidslinks.com/SSEL/feel